What Are CBDC's?

Exploring Central Bank Digital Currencies

Exploring the Future of Digital Currencies

I0490931

By Hugh Webb

Disclaimer:

The information provided in this book is for educational and informational purposes only. The author is not a licensed professional, and the content should not be considered a substitute for professional advice or services. The reader assumes full responsibility for any actions taken based on the information in this book. The author and publisher are not liable for any damages or negative consequences arising from the use or misuse of the information provided. It is recommended that readers conduct their own research and consult with a professional before making any significant changes to their cleaning routine or use of natural cleaning products.

Table of Contents

Chapter 1: Definition of CBDC's and their Significance in the Global Financial Landscape

Central Bank Digital Currency (CBDC) is a type of digital currency that is issued and backed by a country's central bank. CBDC's are a new form of digital currency that can be used to make payments, store value, and transfer funds. Unlike cryptocurrencies, which are not backed by any central authority, CBDC's are backed by the full faith and credit of the central bank, which gives them a degree of stability and trustworthiness that other digital currencies may lack.

The significance of CBDC's in the global financial landscape is immense. For one, they have the potential to transform the way we use money and make payments. With CBDC's, payments can be made more quickly, cheaply, and securely than with traditional currencies. This could have a profound impact on the financial industry, reducing the need for intermediaries and speeding up settlement times.

CBDC's also have the potential to increase financial inclusion. In many parts of the world, people lack access to basic financial services such as bank accounts or credit. CBDC's could provide a way for these people to participate in the financial system and access the benefits it offers.

CBDC's also have the potential to reduce the risk of fraud and money laundering. Because CBDC's are digital, they can be traced more easily than physical cash, making it harder for criminals to engage in illegal activities.

Finally, CBDC's could have implications for monetary policy. Central banks could use CBDC's to implement monetary policy more effectively, for example by adjusting interest rates or changing the money supply in real-time.

Overall, CBDC's represent an exciting new development in the global financial landscape. While there are still many questions and concerns surrounding their implementation, their potential benefits are clear. As central banks around the world explore the possibilities of CBDC's, it will be interesting to see how they develop and evolve over time.

Chapter 2: Brief Overview of the History of Digital Currencies

Digital currencies have a relatively short history, with the first digital currency, eCash, being introduced in the 1980s by cryptographer David Chaum. eCash was a digital version of cash that allowed users to make anonymous transactions online. It was used for a brief period of time, but ultimately failed due to a lack of widespread adoption.

In the late 1990s, a new digital currency called Beenz was introduced. Beenz was a loyalty currency that could be earned and redeemed on participating websites. While it had some success, it ultimately failed due to a lack of demand.

The first successful digital currency was Bitcoin, which was introduced in 2009 by an anonymous person or group known as Satoshi Nakamoto. Bitcoin was designed to be a decentralized digital currency that could be used for peer-to-peer transactions without the need for intermediaries like banks. It quickly gained popularity among early adopters and has since become the most widely known and used digital currency.

Since the introduction of Bitcoin, thousands of other digital currencies, known as altcoins, have been created. Many of these altcoins have been designed to address perceived flaws in Bitcoin, such as its slow transaction times and high fees. Some of the most popular altcoins include Ethereum, Litecoin, and Ripple.

In addition to digital currencies, blockchain technology, the technology behind many digital currencies, has also gained popularity. Blockchain is a decentralized ledger that records all transactions in a secure and transparent manner. It has the potential to transform many industries, including finance, healthcare, and supply chain management.

While digital currencies and blockchain technology are still relatively new, their potential impact is significant. They have the potential to transform the way we do business, make payments, and store value. As technology continues to evolve, it will be interesting to see how digital currencies and blockchain continue to develop and shape the global financial landscape.

Chapter 3: Importance of CBDC's in the Context of the COVID-19 Pandemic

The COVID-19 pandemic has had a profound impact on the global economy, with many countries experiencing significant disruptions to their financial systems. In this context, CBDC's have emerged as an important tool for central banks and governments to help manage the economic fallout from the pandemic.

One of the key benefits of CBDC's in the context of the pandemic is their potential to enable contactless payments. With many people avoiding physical contact and cash transactions due to the risk of transmitting the virus, CBDC's can provide a safe and convenient way for people to make payments without the need for physical cash or credit cards.

CBDC's can also help governments distribute stimulus payments more quickly and efficiently. In many countries, governments have implemented stimulus packages to help support individuals and businesses affected by the pandemic. With CBDC's, these payments can be distributed directly to individuals' digital wallets, eliminating the need for intermediaries and reducing the risk of fraud or errors.

CBDC's can also help central banks manage the money supply more effectively. With the pandemic leading to significant disruptions in supply chains and economic activity, central banks need to be able to respond quickly and adjust monetary policy as needed. CBDC's can provide a way for central banks to do this more effectively, enabling them to make real-time adjustments to interest rates, money supply, and other key economic indicators.

Finally, CBDC's can help increase financial inclusion and support vulnerable populations during the pandemic. With many people facing job losses and other economic challenges, CBDC's can provide a way for them to access financial services and support. CBDC's can also help facilitate international transactions and reduce the cost and complexity of cross-border payments.

Overall, CBDC's have emerged as an important tool in the context of the COVID-19 pandemic. While their implementation is still in the early stages, their potential to support economic recovery and help manage the impact of the pandemic is significant. As governments and central banks around the world continue to explore the possibilities of CBDC's, it will be interesting to see how they are integrated into the global financial landscape.

Chapter 4: The Role of Central Banks in Issuing CBDC's

Central banks play a critical role in the issuance and management of CBDC's. As the institutions responsible for managing monetary policy and maintaining financial stability, central banks have the expertise and infrastructure necessary to ensure the safe and effective implementation of CBDC's.

One of the key responsibilities of central banks in issuing CBDC's is ensuring that they are designed and implemented in a way that aligns with their overall monetary policy objectives. CBDC's can be designed to serve a variety of purposes, such as improving financial inclusion, increasing the efficiency of payments, and reducing the risk of fraud and money laundering. Central banks need to carefully consider these objectives and design CBDC's that support their overall monetary policy goals.

Central banks also need to ensure that CBDC's are designed in a way that promotes financial stability and minimizes risks to the financial system. This includes ensuring that CBDC's are secure, resistant to hacking and other forms of cyber attacks, and designed to minimize the risk of fraud and money laundering. Central banks also need to consider the potential impact of CBDC's on the broader financial system, including the potential for CBDC's to displace existing forms of money and the potential for CBDC's to increase systemic risk.

Another key role of central banks in issuing CBDC's is managing the infrastructure necessary to support them. This includes designing and implementing the necessary technological infrastructure, such as the blockchain or other distributed ledger technologies, to enable the issuance and management of CBDC's. Central banks also need to ensure that the necessary legal and regulatory frameworks are in place to support the issuance and use of CBDC's.

Finally, central banks need to ensure that the issuance of CBDC's is transparent and accountable. This includes providing clear guidance on the issuance and use of CBDC's, as well as ensuring that the necessary governance structures are in place to ensure the effective management of CBDC's.

Overall, central banks play a critical role in the issuance and management of CBDC's. As the institutions responsible for maintaining financial stability and managing monetary policy, central banks have the expertise and infrastructure necessary to ensure the safe and effective implementation of CBDC's.

Chapter 5: Definition of CBDC's and How They Differ from Traditional Currencies

A Central Bank Digital Currency (CBDC) is a digital form of fiat currency issued by a central bank. Unlike traditional currencies, which are physical notes and coins, CBDC's exist entirely in digital form and are typically based on blockchain or other distributed ledger technologies.

One of the key differences between CBDC's and traditional currencies is the way they are issued and managed. Traditional currencies are issued by central banks and distributed through commercial banks and other financial institutions. In contrast, CBDC's are issued directly by central banks and can be held by individuals and businesses in digital wallets.

Another difference between CBDC's and traditional currencies is the way they are stored and transferred. Traditional currencies are typically stored in bank accounts or physical wallets and transferred through intermediaries such as banks and payment processors. CBDC's, on the other hand, are stored in digital wallets and can be transferred directly between individuals and businesses.

CBDC's also have the potential to offer a range of benefits that traditional currencies do not. For example, CBDC's can provide greater financial inclusion by allowing individuals and businesses who are underserved by traditional financial institutions to access financial services. CBDC's can also offer faster and more efficient payment processing, lower transaction costs, and greater transparency and security.

However, CBDC's also pose a number of challenges and risks that need to be carefully considered. For example, the design and implementation of CBDC's need to be carefully managed to ensure that they do not pose a threat to financial stability or increase the risk of money laundering or other illegal activities.

Overall, CBDC's represent an innovative and potentially transformative development in the global financial landscape. As central banks and governments around the world continue to explore the possibilities of CBDC's, it will be important to carefully consider the potential benefits and risks associated with this new form of digital currency.

Chapter 6: Different Types of CBDC's and Their Characteristics

There are several different types of CBDC's that central banks can issue, each with its own unique characteristics and potential benefits.

1. Retail CBDC's: Retail CBDC's are designed to be used by individuals and businesses for everyday transactions, such as buying goods and services. Retail CBDC's are typically held in digital wallets and can be used to make instant payments and transfers, as well as to store value. Retail CBDC's can offer a range of benefits, including faster and more efficient payment processing, greater financial inclusion, and improved security and transparency.

2. Wholesale CBDC's: Wholesale CBDC's are designed for use by financial institutions and other large-scale users, such as corporations and governments. Wholesale CBDC's are typically used for large-value transactions and can be settled instantly and securely. Wholesale CBDC's can offer a range of benefits, including lower transaction costs, reduced settlement risk, and increased efficiency in the financial system.

3. Hybrid CBDC's: Hybrid CBDC's combine elements of both retail and wholesale CBDC's. Hybrid CBDC's can be used for both small-scale retail transactions and large-scale wholesale transactions, providing a flexible and adaptable form of digital currency. Hybrid CBDC's can offer a range of benefits, including greater versatility and flexibility, improved efficiency in the financial system, and increased financial inclusion.

4. Token-Based CBDC's: Token-based CBDC's are based on blockchain or other distributed ledger technologies and use cryptographic tokens to represent digital currency. Token-based CBDC's can offer a range of benefits, including improved security and transparency, increased efficiency in payment processing, and greater interoperability with other blockchain-based systems.
5. Account-Based CBDC's: Account-based CBDC's are similar to traditional bank accounts, with central banks holding and managing the digital currency on behalf of individuals and businesses. Account-based CBDC's can offer a range of benefits, including increased security and transparency, reduced transaction costs, and improved financial inclusion.

Overall, the choice of CBDC type will depend on the specific needs and objectives of central banks and the wider financial system. Each type of CBDC has its own unique characteristics and potential benefits, and central banks will need to carefully consider these factors when deciding which type of CBDC to issue.

Chapter 7: Overview of Countries that have Launched or are Testing CBDC's

In recent years, a growing number of central banks around the world have been exploring the potential of CBDC's and developing their own digital currencies. Here is an overview of some of the countries that have launched or are testing CBDC's:

1. China: The People's Bank of China has been developing a digital currency called the Digital Currency Electronic Payment (DCEP) since 2014. The DCEP has already been piloted in several major cities, and is expected to be rolled out more widely in the coming years.
2. Sweden: The Riksbank, Sweden's central bank, has been exploring the potential of an e-krona since 2017. The Riksbank has already conducted a successful pilot of the e-krona, and is now moving forward with plans to develop and test a more advanced version of the digital currency.
3. The Bahamas: The Central Bank of The Bahamas launched the Sand Dollar in 2020, making it one of the first countries in the world to issue a CBDC. The Sand Dollar is currently being used in a number of pilot programs across the country.
4. Uruguay: The Central Bank of Uruguay has been testing a digital currency called e-Peso since 2018. The e-Peso is designed to be used for small-scale retail transactions, and has already been used in a number of successful pilots.
5. Japan: The Bank of Japan has been exploring the potential of CBDC's since 2018, and has recently launched a proof-of-concept test to evaluate the feasibility of a digital yen.

6. The European Union: The European Central Bank has been exploring the potential of a digital euro since 2019, and is currently conducting a public consultation to gather feedback on the design and implementation of the digital currency.

These are just a few examples of the many countries that are currently exploring the potential of CBDC's. As central banks around the world continue to develop and test digital currencies, it is clear that CBDC's are likely to become an increasingly important feature of the global financial landscape in the years to come.

Chapter 8: Comparison of CBDC's in Different Regions

As central banks around the world explore the potential of CBDC's, it is becoming increasingly clear that different regions may take different approaches to the design and implementation of digital currencies. Here is a comparison of some of the key features of CBDC's in different regions:

Asia:

Several countries in Asia, including China and Japan, are among the most advanced in their development of CBDC's. These countries are focused on using digital currencies to increase financial inclusion, improve the efficiency of payments systems, and reduce the dependence on traditional financial institutions. In general, CBDC's in Asia tend to be more centralized and tightly controlled by the government.

Europe:

The European Union has been exploring the potential of a digital euro since 2019, and is currently conducting a public consultation to gather feedback on the design and implementation of the digital currency. In general, CBDC's in Europe are more focused on promoting innovation and competition in the financial sector, and are designed to work in conjunction with existing payment systems.

Americas:

The Americas are home to a number of countries that are exploring the potential of CBDC's, including the United States, Canada, and Brazil. These countries are generally focused on using digital currencies to improve the efficiency of payments systems, reduce transaction costs, and increase financial inclusion. In general, CBDC's in the Americas tend to be more decentralized and market-oriented than in Asia.

In conclusion, while there are some common themes among CBDC's in different regions, there are also significant differences in terms of their design, objectives, and implementation. As more countries around the world move forward with the development of digital currencies, it will be important to monitor these differences and evaluate their impact on the global financial landscape.

Chapter 9: Potential Impact of CBDC's on International Trade and Financial Stability

The emergence of CBDC's has the potential to have a significant impact on the global financial landscape, particularly in the areas of international trade and financial stability. Here are some potential impacts of CBDC's on these areas:

International Trade:
1. Increased Efficiency: CBDC's could increase the efficiency of cross-border payments and reduce the time and cost associated with international trade. This could be particularly beneficial for small and medium-sized enterprises (SMEs) that may not have access to traditional banking services.
2. Reduced Dependence on the U.S. Dollar: As more countries develop and adopt their own CBDC's, there may be a reduced reliance on the U.S. dollar as the dominant currency for international trade.
3. Increased Competition: CBDC's could increase competition in the payments industry and reduce the market dominance of traditional financial institutions.

Financial Stability:
1. Increased Financial Inclusion: CBDC's could increase financial inclusion by providing access to digital currencies to individuals who may not have access to traditional banking services.
2. Reduced Risks: CBDC's could reduce risks associated with traditional payment systems, such as counterparty risk and settlement risk.
3. Enhanced Central Bank Control: CBDC's could enhance the control of central banks over the money supply, potentially reducing the risk of inflation or deflation.

However, there are also potential risks associated with the development and adoption of CBDC's, including the risk of cyber-attacks and the potential for financial disintermediation. As such, it will be important for central banks and policymakers to carefully consider the potential risks and benefits of CBDC's as they move forward with their development and implementation.

In conclusion, while CBDC's have the potential to revolutionize the way we think about money and payments, it is important to carefully consider their potential impacts on international trade and financial stability, and to work to mitigate any potential risks.

Chapter 10: Overview of Blockchain Technology and its Relevance to CBDC's

Blockchain technology is a decentralized digital ledger that allows for the secure and transparent recording of transactions. It is the underlying technology behind many cryptocurrencies, including Bitcoin and Ethereum, and has gained widespread attention for its potential to revolutionize the financial industry. Here is an overview of blockchain technology and its relevance to CBDC's:

1. Decentralization: One of the key features of blockchain technology is its decentralized nature, which means that there is no single central authority controlling the ledger. This makes it a promising technology for CBDC's, which could potentially be designed to be decentralized and provide greater financial inclusion.
2. Security: Blockchain technology is highly secure due to its use of cryptographic algorithms to verify transactions. This makes it difficult for bad actors to manipulate the ledger, which is a critical requirement for any digital currency.
3. Transparency: Another key feature of blockchain technology is its transparency, which means that all transactions are visible to everyone on the network. This could be a useful feature for CBDC's, as it could enhance the public's trust in the currency and provide greater accountability.
4. Programmability: Blockchain technology is highly programmable, which means that it can be used to create smart contracts and other automated financial instruments. This could be a useful feature for CBDC's, as it could enable the development of new financial products and services.

While blockchain technology has many potential benefits for CBDC's, there are also some challenges that need to be addressed, such as scalability, energy consumption, and interoperability. As such, it will be important for central banks and policymakers to carefully consider the potential benefits and risks of blockchain technology as they move forward with the development of CBDC's.

In conclusion, blockchain technology is a promising technology for CBDC's, as it has the potential to provide greater security, transparency, and decentralization. As central banks and policymakers continue to explore the potential of CBDC's, it will be important to carefully consider the potential benefits and risks of blockchain technology and to design CBDC's in a way that maximizes their potential while minimizing any potential risks.

Chapter 11: Comparison of Different Blockchain Platforms for CBDC's

As central banks around the world explore the potential of CBDC's, one of the key decisions they will need to make is which blockchain platform to use. There are many different blockchain platforms available, each with their own strengths and weaknesses. Here is a comparison of some of the most popular blockchain platforms for CBDC's:

1. Ethereum: Ethereum is a popular blockchain platform that is highly programmable and supports the development of decentralized applications (dApps). It has a large and active community of developers, which makes it an attractive option for CBDC's. However, its high gas fees and scalability issues may make it less suitable for large-scale CBDC deployments.
2. Hyperledger Fabric: Hyperledger Fabric is a permissioned blockchain platform that is designed for enterprise use cases. It is highly scalable and customizable, which makes it an attractive option for CBDC's. However, it may be less suitable for public CBDC's that require greater decentralization.
3. Corda: Corda is a permissioned blockchain platform that is designed for use in financial services. It is highly scalable and supports confidential transactions, which makes it a good option for CBDC's that require privacy and security. However, its focus on financial services may make it less suitable for CBDC's that need to serve a wider range of use cases.

4. Stellar: Stellar is a public blockchain platform that is designed for payments. It is highly scalable and supports fast transactions, which makes it an attractive option for CBDC's that need to support high transaction volumes. However, its focus on payments may make it less suitable for CBDC's that need to support more complex financial instruments.
5. Ripple: Ripple is a permissioned blockchain platform that is designed for cross-border payments. It is highly scalable and supports fast transactions, which makes it an attractive option for CBDC's that need to support international payments. However, its centralized nature may make it less suitable for public CBDC's that require greater decentralization.

Ultimately, the choice of blockchain platform for CBDC's will depend on a range of factors, including the specific use case, the level of decentralization required, and the scalability and security needs of the system. As central banks and policymakers continue to explore the potential of CBDC's, they will need to carefully consider these factors and choose a blockchain platform that best meets their needs.

Chapter 12: The Role of Smart Contracts and Digital Identity in CBDC's

CBDC's have the potential to transform the way we think about money and financial transactions. Two key technologies that are likely to play a central role in CBDC's are smart contracts and digital identity.

Smart contracts are self-executing contracts with the terms of the agreement between buyer and seller being directly written into lines of code. They can automate complex financial transactions, such as escrow agreements and cross-border payments. Smart contracts can also be used to enforce compliance with regulations and to ensure that transactions are transparent and tamper-proof.

Digital identity is another technology that is likely to play a key role in CBDC's. Digital identity refers to the collection of information that identifies a person or entity in the digital world. Digital identity can be used to verify the identity of participants in financial transactions and to prevent fraud and money laundering.

Together, smart contracts and digital identity can help to create a more efficient and secure financial system. For example, smart contracts can be used to automate compliance with know-your-customer (KYC) and anti-money laundering (AML) regulations, reducing the burden on financial institutions and improving the accuracy of compliance processes. Digital identity can be used to ensure that only authorized participants are able to access and use CBDC's, reducing the risk of fraud and misuse.

However, there are also challenges associated with the use of smart contracts and digital identity in CBDC's. One challenge is ensuring the privacy and security of personal data. Another challenge is ensuring that smart contracts are reliable and enforceable, particularly in complex financial transactions.

Despite these challenges, the potential benefits of smart contracts and digital identity are significant. As central banks and policymakers continue to explore the potential of CBDC's, they will need to carefully consider how to incorporate these technologies into CBDC's in a way that maximizes their benefits while minimizing their risks. By doing so, CBDC's have the potential to transform the way we think about money and financial transactions, creating a more efficient, secure, and transparent financial system.

Chapter 13: The Role of Government and Regulatory Bodies in Implementing CBDC's

The implementation of CBDC's involves not only the central banks but also the government and regulatory bodies. These institutions play a critical role in ensuring that CBDC's are implemented in a safe and efficient manner and that they comply with relevant laws and regulations.

One key role of government and regulatory bodies is to ensure that CBDC's do not undermine financial stability or pose a risk to the broader economy. CBDC's could potentially disrupt the existing financial system and the role of banks, so it is important for governments to carefully consider the potential impacts of CBDC's and to develop policies and regulations that mitigate risks.

Governments also have a role in ensuring that CBDC's are accessible to everyone, including individuals and businesses that are currently underserved by the traditional banking system. CBDC's have the potential to reduce the reliance on cash and to increase financial inclusion, but it is important for governments to ensure that CBDC's are designed with this goal in mind.

Another role of government and regulatory bodies is to ensure that CBDC's are secure and that they comply with relevant laws and regulations. This includes ensuring that CBDC's are not used for illegal activities such as money laundering and terrorism financing, and that they protect the privacy of users.

Regulatory bodies also have a role in overseeing the development of CBDC's and ensuring that they are interoperable with other payment systems. Interoperability is important for ensuring that CBDC's can be used across borders and that they can work with other payment systems to create a seamless global financial system.

In addition, governments and regulatory bodies play a role in promoting innovation and competition in the development of CBDC's. By creating a supportive regulatory environment, governments can encourage the development of new technologies and business models that can help to improve the efficiency and accessibility of financial services.

Overall, the role of government and regulatory bodies in implementing CBDC's is critical. By working together with central banks and other stakeholders, governments can help to ensure that CBDC's are implemented in a safe and efficient manner, that they promote financial inclusion, and that they comply with relevant laws and regulations.

Chapter 14: Implications for Monetary Policy and Financial Stability

The introduction of CBDC's has significant implications for monetary policy and financial stability. CBDC's represent a new form of money that is backed by the central bank and can potentially be used by anyone with a digital device, bypassing traditional banks and payment systems. This has the potential to fundamentally change the way that money is created and circulated in the economy.

One potential implication of CBDC's for monetary policy is that they could make it easier for central banks to implement monetary policy. With CBDC's, central banks can potentially implement negative interest rates directly on accounts, rather than relying on banks to pass on rate cuts to customers. This could provide more flexibility for monetary policy and help to stimulate economic activity during periods of low inflation or recession.

Another potential implication of CBDC's for monetary policy is that they could change the demand for traditional bank deposits, potentially reducing the need for banks to rely on wholesale funding markets. This could make banks more resilient to funding shocks, but it could also reduce their profitability and lead to changes in the structure of the banking system.

CBDC's also have implications for financial stability. One potential risk is that they could lead to a flight of deposits from traditional banks, particularly if CBDC's offer higher interest rates or are seen as a safer alternative to traditional bank deposits. This could potentially destabilize the banking system and lead to a loss of confidence in traditional banks.

Another potential risk is that CBDC's could increase the risk of financial cyberattacks and other security risks. As CBDC's become more widely used, they could become an attractive target for hackers and other malicious actors, potentially leading to disruptions in the financial system.

To mitigate these risks, central banks and other regulators will need to carefully monitor the development of CBDC's and ensure that they are designed in a way that promotes financial stability and resilience. This may involve setting limits on the amount of CBDC's that can be held by any one individual or institution, as well as implementing strict security measures to prevent cyberattacks and other security breaches.

Overall, the introduction of CBDC's has significant implications for monetary policy and financial stability. While CBDC's have the potential to increase financial inclusion and improve the efficiency of the financial system, they also pose significant risks and challenges that must be carefully managed by central banks and other regulators.

Chapter 15: Privacy and Security Concerns Surrounding CBDC's

The development of CBDC's has raised concerns about privacy and security. CBDC's have the potential to provide greater financial inclusion and efficiency, but they also raise questions about how user data will be collected and stored, and how it will be protected from cyber threats and other security risks.

Privacy Concerns:

One concern is that the use of CBDC's could potentially enable the government or central bank to monitor individuals' transactions and financial activity. This could raise privacy concerns, particularly if the data is used for purposes other than monetary policy or financial stability.

To address these concerns, some CBDC projects have been designed with privacy features that limit the amount of data that is collected and stored. For example, some CBDC's use a 'digital cash' model, where transactions are anonymous and do not reveal the identity of the parties involved.

However, there is a trade-off between privacy and transparency. In order to prevent money laundering and other illicit activities, regulators may need to have some level of visibility into transactions. Finding a balance between privacy and transparency will be a key challenge for CBDC projects.

Security Concerns:

CBDC's also raise security concerns, particularly in relation to cyber threats. As CBDC's become more widely used, they could become a target for hackers and other malicious actors, who could attempt to steal user data or manipulate transactions.

To address these concerns, CBDC projects must be designed with strong security measures, including encryption and multi-factor authentication. In addition, central banks and other regulators will need to monitor CBDC transactions for signs of fraud or other illegal activity.

Another potential security concern is the risk of centralization. CBDC's are backed by the central bank, which means that they are ultimately controlled by a single entity. This could potentially make CBDC's more vulnerable to political interference or other external pressures.

To mitigate this risk, some CBDC projects have been designed with decentralized features, such as using blockchain technology to distribute control and decision-making across a network of nodes. This could potentially make CBDC's more resistant to external pressures and more resilient in the face of cyber threats.

Conclusion:

Privacy and security concerns are important considerations for the development of CBDC's. While CBDC's have the potential to provide greater financial inclusion and efficiency, they also raise questions about how user data will be collected and stored, and how it will be protected from cyber threats and other security risks. Finding a balance between privacy and transparency, and designing CBDC's with strong security measures, will be key to ensuring that CBDC's can be used safely and securely.

Chapter 16: Potential Impact of CBDC's on the Financial Industry

The emergence of CBDC's has the potential to transform the financial industry in a number of ways, from improving payment systems to creating new business opportunities. In this chapter, we will explore some of the potential impacts of CBDC's on the financial industry.

Improved Payment Systems

One of the main advantages of CBDC's is that they could provide a more efficient and secure means of payment. CBDC's could be used to facilitate instant and low-cost cross-border payments, which would be particularly beneficial for small and medium-sized businesses that currently face high fees and lengthy processing times.

In addition, CBDC's could potentially eliminate the need for intermediaries such as payment processors, which would reduce transaction costs and improve the speed of payments. This could also have implications for the banking industry, as banks currently generate significant revenue from payment processing fees.

New Business Opportunities

CBDC's could also create new business opportunities in areas such as digital identity, smart contracts, and decentralized finance (DeFi). For example, CBDC's could be used to facilitate secure and efficient digital identity verification, which would be particularly useful for industries such as healthcare and online retail.

In addition, CBDC's could enable the use of smart contracts, which are self-executing contracts that automate the transfer of assets based on predefined conditions. This could potentially revolutionize industries such as real estate and supply chain management, by streamlining transactions and reducing the need for intermediaries.

Finally, CBDC's could pave the way for the growth of DeFi, which is a decentralized financial system that operates on blockchain technology. DeFi has the potential to provide greater financial inclusion and transparency, by enabling anyone with an internet connection to access financial services.

Disruption of the Banking Industry

The emergence of CBDC's could also have significant implications for the banking industry. As CBDC's become more widely used, they could potentially displace traditional banks as the primary provider of financial services.

This could happen if CBDC's are designed to be accessible to individuals and businesses without the need for a bank account. In this scenario, banks would no longer have a monopoly on financial services, and could face significant competition from other players in the market.

However, it is important to note that this scenario is not inevitable. Banks could adapt to the emergence of CBDC's by developing new products and services that complement CBDC's, such as offering value-added services such as financial advice and wealth management.

Conclusion

CBDC's have the potential to transform the financial industry by improving payment systems, creating new business opportunities, and potentially disrupting the banking industry. However, the extent of these impacts will depend on a range of factors, including the design of CBDC's, the regulatory environment, and the response of market players such as banks and fintech companies.

Chapter 17: Opportunities for Innovation and Financial Inclusion

Central bank digital currencies (CBDCs) have the potential to revolutionize the financial landscape by increasing financial inclusion and fostering innovation. CBDCs can help in addressing the challenges faced by traditional financial systems, such as high transaction fees, lack of transparency, and limited access to financial services. In this chapter, we will discuss the opportunities for innovation and financial inclusion that CBDCs present.

Financial Inclusion

One of the main advantages of CBDCs is the potential to increase financial inclusion. CBDCs can provide a safe and accessible means for people to store and transfer money, even if they do not have access to traditional banking services. For example, in many developing countries, a significant portion of the population is unbanked or underbanked. CBDCs can help bridge the gap by providing a low-cost and secure means of making payments and storing value.

In addition, CBDCs can help reduce the reliance on cash, which can be expensive to produce and manage. By providing a digital alternative to physical cash, CBDCs can improve the efficiency of payments and reduce the cost of cash handling for governments and businesses.

Opportunities for Innovation

CBDCs can also foster innovation in the financial industry. CBDCs can be programmed with smart contracts, which can automate financial transactions and enable new business models. Smart contracts can also enable the creation of decentralized financial applications, such as decentralized exchanges and lending platforms, which can operate without the need for intermediaries.

CBDCs can also facilitate cross-border payments, which can be expensive and time-consuming. By providing a digital alternative to traditional cross-border payments, CBDCs can reduce transaction costs and improve the speed and efficiency of cross-border transactions.

In addition, CBDCs can provide greater transparency and traceability in financial transactions, which can help prevent fraud and financial crime. CBDCs can also provide real-time data on the use of money, which can help central banks and other regulatory authorities make informed decisions about monetary policy and financial stability.

Conclusion

CBDCs have the potential to revolutionize the financial landscape by increasing financial inclusion and fostering innovation. CBDCs can provide a safe and accessible means for people to store and transfer money, even if they do not have access to traditional banking services. CBDCs can also facilitate cross-border payments, automate financial transactions, and enable new business models. However, to fully realize the potential of CBDCs, it is important to address the challenges of privacy and security, and ensure that regulatory frameworks are in place to support their use.

Chapter 18: Potential challenges and risks associated with CBDC's

While CBDC's offer several potential benefits, they also pose certain challenges and risks. In this chapter, we will discuss some of the potential challenges and risks associated with CBDC's.

Cybersecurity Risks: CBDC's rely on digital infrastructure, which makes them vulnerable to cyber-attacks. If an attacker gains access to the system, they could potentially manipulate or steal funds. This would require significant investment in cybersecurity measures to ensure the security of the system.

Lack of Anonymity: CBDC's can provide transaction data in real-time, which can help identify criminal activities. However, this also means that users have little to no anonymity when using CBDC's. Governments and other authorities could potentially use this data for surveillance and monitoring purposes, which raises concerns about privacy and civil liberties.

Potential Disruption to Traditional Financial Systems: CBDC's could potentially disrupt traditional financial systems and challenge the role of commercial banks in the economy. If CBDC's become widely adopted, they could reduce the demand for bank deposits and decrease the need for commercial bank lending.

Financial Stability Risks: CBDC's could pose risks to financial stability if they are not implemented and managed appropriately. For instance, if a CBDC is too volatile, it could destabilize the economy and cause economic downturns.

Implementation Challenges: Implementing a CBDC requires significant investment in technology and infrastructure. This investment may be difficult to justify, especially for smaller economies with limited resources.

Adoption and Acceptance: CBDC's require widespread adoption and acceptance to be successful. If consumers and businesses do not see the benefits of CBDC's or if they do not trust the system, it may not gain widespread adoption.

Cross-Border Payments: The interoperability of CBDC's across different countries and regions is a challenge that needs to be addressed. This requires coordination between different central banks, which may not always be possible.

In conclusion, CBDC's offer several potential benefits, but they also pose several challenges and risks. These risks must be addressed to ensure the successful implementation and adoption of CBDC's.

Chapter 19: Summary of key points covered in the book

In this book, we have explored the concept of Central Bank Digital Currencies (CBDC's) and their potential impact on the global financial system. Here are some of the key points covered in this book:

- CBDC's are digital versions of fiat currencies that are issued and backed by central banks.
- CBDC's offer several potential benefits, including increased financial inclusion, improved payment efficiency, and reduced costs.
- There are different types of CBDC's, including retail CBDC's, wholesale CBDC's, and hybrid CBDC's, each with its own characteristics.
- Several countries are already testing or have launched their own CBDC's, including China, Sweden, the Bahamas, and the United States.
- The implementation of CBDC's requires significant investment in technology and infrastructure and requires coordination between central banks, governments, and regulatory bodies.
- Blockchain technology is relevant to CBDC's as it can provide secure and efficient ways of processing transactions.
- Privacy and security concerns must be addressed when implementing CBDC's to ensure the protection of user data and funds.
- CBDC's pose several challenges and risks, including cybersecurity risks, lack of anonymity, potential disruption to traditional financial systems, financial stability risks, implementation challenges, adoption and acceptance, and cross-border payment interoperability.

Overall, CBDC's have the potential to transform the global financial system, but their implementation requires careful consideration of the challenges and risks associated with them.

Chapter 20: The dangers of using CBDC's

While Central Bank Digital Currencies (CBDC's) offer potential benefits, they also pose some significant dangers. Here are some key dangers associated with the use of CBDC's:

1. Cybersecurity risks: The use of CBDC's increases the risk of cyber-attacks, as they are digital and can be accessed remotely. Cyber criminals can hack into systems and steal digital currency, potentially causing significant financial losses.
2. Financial stability risks: CBDC's have the potential to destabilize the financial system if not properly managed. The large-scale adoption of CBDC's could potentially lead to a rapid shift away from traditional bank deposits, leading to liquidity problems and financial instability.
3. Reduced privacy: CBDC's may be more traceable than cash transactions, reducing privacy for users. Governments may be able to track and monitor transactions, potentially leading to surveillance and invasion of privacy.
4. Potential loss of monetary control: The use of CBDC's could potentially lead to a loss of monetary control for central banks. This is because CBDC's are decentralized and could be subject to market forces that are difficult to control, potentially leading to inflation or deflation.
5. Technological risks: CBDC's rely on complex technology that is subject to failures, glitches, and hacking. Technical issues could potentially lead to losses of funds or the inability to transact.
6. Social risks: The use of CBDC's could potentially exacerbate social and economic inequalities, as they may require access to technology and the internet. This could lead to financial exclusion for those who do not have access to technology, creating a digital divide.

It is important to carefully consider these dangers and take steps to mitigate them before implementing CBDC's. Governments and central banks must ensure that the necessary infrastructure and regulatory frameworks are in place to minimize risks and ensure the successful adoption and operation of CBDC's. Additionally, ongoing monitoring and risk assessment is essential to ensure that the potential dangers of CBDC's are properly managed.

Chapter 21: Final thoughts on the future of CBDC's and their potential impact on the global economy

Central Bank Digital Currencies (CBDC's) have the potential to transform the global financial system and impact the global economy in several ways. Here are some final thoughts on the future of CBDC's and their potential impact:

- CBDC's could potentially improve financial inclusion, especially in developing countries where access to banking services is limited.
- The implementation of CBDC's could potentially lead to significant changes in the banking industry, including the displacement of traditional banking services and the emergence of new players in the financial services sector.
- CBDC's could potentially enhance the effectiveness of monetary policy, enabling central banks to better control inflation and manage the money supply.
- The use of CBDC's could potentially increase the efficiency of cross-border payments and reduce costs associated with international transfers.
- CBDC's could potentially enhance the transparency and security of financial transactions, reducing the risks of fraud and corruption.
- CBDC's could potentially reduce the dependence on cash, leading to a more efficient and streamlined payment system.
- The use of CBDC's could potentially pose challenges to privacy and data protection, requiring careful consideration of regulatory frameworks to ensure the protection of user data.

Overall, CBDC's have the potential to transform the global financial system, leading to significant changes in the banking industry and impacting the global economy in several ways. Their implementation requires careful consideration of the challenges and risks associated with them, and effective regulatory frameworks must be put in place to ensure their successful adoption and operation. As the technology and infrastructure supporting CBDC's continue to develop, it will be important to monitor their impact on the global economy and adjust policies as needed to ensure their continued success.

Epilogue:

In conclusion, the rise of CBDCs marks an exciting new chapter in the evolution of money and finance. While there are many questions and challenges surrounding the adoption of these digital currencies, there is no doubt that they have the potential to transform the financial landscape in significant ways.

As we move towards a more digitized and interconnected world, it is essential to stay informed about the latest developments in digital finance. CBDCs are just one example of the technological innovations that are shaping the future of money, and it's important to keep an open mind and a willingness to learn.

Ultimately, the success of CBDCs will depend on a range of factors, including regulatory frameworks, technological infrastructure, and public acceptance. However, with careful planning and collaboration between government, businesses, and consumers, CBDCs could become a powerful tool for promoting financial inclusion, improving efficiency, and unlocking new opportunities for growth and prosperity.

As we look towards the future, it's clear that digital currencies will continue to play an increasingly important role in the global economy. Whether you're a policymaker, a business leader, or simply someone who's interested in the world of finance, there has never been a more exciting time to explore the potential of CBDCs and other digital currencies.